Poptropica

MAD LIBS

concept created by Roger Price & Leonard Stern

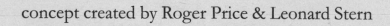

PSS!

PRICE STERN SLOAN

An Imprint of Penguin Group (USA) Inc.

PRICE STERN SLOAN
Published by the Penguin Group
Penguin Group (USA) Inc., 375 Hudson Street, New York, New York 10014, USA
Penguin Group (Canada), 90 Eglinton Avenue East, Suite 700,
Toronto, Ontario M4P 2Y3, Canada
(a division of Pearson Penguin Canada Inc.)
Penguin Books Ltd., 80 Strand, London WC2R 0RL, England
Penguin Group Ireland, 25 St. Stephen's Green, Dublin 2, Ireland
(a division of Penguin Books Ltd.)
Penguin Group (Australia), 250 Camberwell Road, Camberwell, Victoria 3124, Australia
(a division of Pearson Australia Group Pty. Ltd.)
Penguin Books India Pvt. Ltd., 11 Community Centre,
Panchsheel Park, New Delhi—110 017, India
Penguin Group (NZ), 67 Apollo Drive, Rosedale, Auckland 0632, New Zealand
(a division of Pearson New Zealand Ltd.)
Penguin Books (South Africa) (Pty.) Ltd., 24 Sturdee Avenue,
Rosebank, Johannesburg 2196, South Africa

Penguin Books Ltd., Registered Offices:
80 Strand, London WC2R 0RL, England

ISBN 978-0-8431-7233-1

3 5 7 9 10 8 6 4 2

MAD LIBS

INSTRUCTIONS

MAD LIBS® is a game for people who don't like games!
It can be played by one, two, three, four, or forty.

• RIDICULOUSLY SIMPLE DIRECTIONS

In this tablet you will find stories containing blank spaces where words are left out. One player, the READER, selects one of these stories. The READER does not tell anyone what the story is about. Instead, he/she asks the other players, the WRITERS, to give him/her words. These words are used to fill in the blank spaces in the story.

• TO PLAY

The READER asks each WRITER in turn to call out a word—an adjective or a noun or whatever the space calls for—and uses them to fill in the blank spaces in the story. The result is a MAD LIBS® game.

When the READER then reads the completed MAD LIBS® game to the other players, they will discover that they have written a story that is fantastic, screamingly funny, shocking, silly, crazy, or just plain dumb—depending upon which words each WRITER called out.

• EXAMPLE (*Before* and *After*)

"_____!" he said _____
  EXCLAMATION   ADVERB

as he jumped into his convertible _____ and
              NOUN

drove off with his _____ wife.
      ADJECTIVE

"*Ouch*!" he said *Stupidly*
  EXCLAMATION   ADVERB

as he jumped into his convertible *cat* and
          NOUN

drove off with his *brave* wife.
     ADJECTIVE

In case you have forgotten what adjectives, adverbs, nouns, and verbs are, here is a quick review:

An ADJECTIVE describes something or somebody. *Lumpy*, *soft*, *ugly*, *messy*, and *short* are adjectives.

An ADVERB tells how something is done. It modifies a verb and usually ends in "ly." *Modestly*, *stupidly*, *greedily*, and *carefully* are adverbs.

A NOUN is the name of a person, place, or thing. *Sidewalk*, *umbrella*, *bridle*, *bathtub*, and *nose* are nouns.

A VERB is an action word. *Run*, *pitch*, *jump*, and *swim* are verbs. Put the verbs in past tense if the directions say PAST TENSE. *Ran*, *pitched*, *jumped*, and *swam* are verbs in the past tense.

When we ask for A PLACE, we mean any sort of place: a country or city (*Spain*, *Cleveland*) or a room (*bathroom*, *kitchen*).

An EXCLAMATION or SILLY WORD is any sort of funny sound, gasp, grunt, or outcry, like *Wow!*, *Ouch!*, *Whomp!*, *Ick!*, and *Gadzooks!*

When we ask for specific words, like a NUMBER, a COLOR, an ANIMAL, or a PART OF THE BODY, we mean a word that is one of those things, like *seven*, *blue*, *horse*, or *head*.

When we ask for a PLURAL, it means more than one. For example, *cat* pluralized is *cats*.

MAD LIBS® is fun to play with friends, but you can also play it by yourself! To begin with, DO NOT look at the story on the page below. Fill in the blanks on this page with the words called for. Then, using the words you have selected, fill in the blank spaces in the story.

Now you've created your own hilarious MAD LIBS® game!

WELCOME TO POPTROPICA

NOUN _____

ADJECTIVE _____

PLURAL NOUN _____

ADJECTIVE _____

ADJECTIVE _____

A PLACE _____

NOUN _____

NOUN _____

NOUN _____

ADJECTIVE _____

VERB _____

PART OF THE BODY _____

PLURAL NOUN _____

CELEBRITY _____

PERSON IN ROOM _____

VERB ENDING IN "ING" _____

A PLACE _____

MAD⊙LIBS®
WELCOME TO POPTROPICA

Does your dream vacation involve relaxing on a sandy

_____ reading a/an _____ book? Or are you the
  NOUN   ADJECTIVE

adventurous type who prefers to battle dangerous _____
                                                  PLURAL NOUN

and hunt _____ creatures? Then forget about romping
          ADJECTIVE

around that _____, all-inclusive resort in (the)
             ADJECTIVE

_____ and join other gamers on a/an _____-filled
 A PLACE   NOUN

journey to Poptropica! You won't travel there by ordinary means,

such as a car, train, or even a winged _____. Instead, you'll
                                         NOUN

soar in a golden _____! Each Island has _____
                  NOUN   ADJECTIVE

challenges to complete. You'll jump, climb, _____, and use
                                             VERB

your supersize _____ to win each quest. Along the way
                PART OF THE BODY

you'll meet questionable _____, like the diabolical scientist
                          PLURAL NOUN

Dr. _____ and the evil pirate leader Captain _____.
     CELEBRITY   PERSON IN ROOM

Best of all, whenever you conquer an Island, you will earn a

medallion—as well as the adoration of millions of cheering,

_____ Poptropicans all across (the) _____!
 VERB ENDING IN "ING"   A PLACE

From POPTROPICA MAD LIBS® • © 2007–2012 Pearson Education, Inc. All rights reserved. Published in 2012
by Price Stern Sloan, a division of Penguin Young Readers Group, 345 Hudson Street, New York, NY 10014.

MAD LIBS® is fun to play with friends, but you can also play it by yourself! To begin with, DO NOT look at the story on the page below. Fill in the blanks on this page with the words called for. Then, using the words you have selected, fill in the blank spaces in the story.

Now you've created your own hilarious MAD LIBS® game!

GAME FACE

ADJECTIVE _____

NOUN _____

COLOR _____

TYPE OF FOOD _____

VERB ENDING IN "ING" _____

ANIMAL _____

ADJECTIVE _____

PART OF THE BODY (PLURAL) _____

PLURAL NOUN _____

PLURAL NOUN _____

ADJECTIVE _____

ADJECTIVE _____

TYPE OF FOOD _____

NOUN _____

NOUN _____

ARTICLE OF CLOTHING _____

PLURAL NOUN _____

NOUN _____

NOUN _____

MAD LIBS

GAME FACE

Every Poptropican has a secret, _____ online identity. Here's
\hfill ADJECTIVE

how to create yours:

1. Choose whether you want to be a boy or a/an _____. You'll
\hfill NOUN

automatically get a cool name like _____ _____
\hfill COLOR \hfill TYPE OF FOOD

or _____ _____.
\hfill VERB ENDING IN "ING" \hfill ANIMAL

2. Not loving your _____ look? It's easy to change your
\hfill ADJECTIVE

appearance, such as the size of your _____ or
\hfill PART OF THE BODY (PLURAL)

the color of the _____ you're wearing.
\hfill PLURAL NOUN

3. Pay a visit to the Poptropica Store. Here you can buy Gold

_____ or _____ costumes. The Gold
\hfill PLURAL NOUN \hfill ADJECTIVE

Cards contain _____ items to have fun with, like
\hfill ADJECTIVE

_____-flavored Popgum that you can chew. Want to
\hfill TYPE OF FOOD

create a style that's half _____ and half _____? Use
\hfill NOUN \hfill NOUN

the Costumizer to copy a look. A character's _____
\hfill ARTICLE OF CLOTHING

with feathered _____ or a sword with a jeweled
\hfill PLURAL NOUN

_____ can be yours with a simple click of the _____!
\hfill NOUN \hfill NOUN

MAD LIBS® is fun to play with friends, but you can also play it by yourself! To begin with, DO NOT look at the story on the page below. Fill in the blanks on this page with the words called for. Then, using the words you have selected, fill in the blank spaces in the story.

Now you've created your own hilarious MAD LIBS® game!

EARLY POPTROPICA: PILGRIM ENCOUNTER

CELEBRITY _____

ADJECTIVE _____

ADJECTIVE _____

ADJECTIVE _____

NOUN _____

TYPE OF LIQUID _____

PLURAL NOUN _____

NOUN _____

ADJECTIVE _____

TYPE OF FOOD (PLURAL) _____

NOUN _____

PLURAL NOUN _____

ADJECTIVE _____

PART OF THE BODY _____

VERB _____

MAD LIBS

EARLY POPTROPICA: PILGRIM ENCOUNTER

Abby Chattypants sat down with Pilgrim _____ for an
                                            CELEBRITY

exclusive interview about the _____ adventures to be
                                  ADJECTIVE

encountered on the Island of Early Poptropica:

Abby: Tell us about the _____ obstacles on this Island.
                                ADJECTIVE

Pilgrim: Visitors to our _____ Island need to locate three
                                 ADJECTIVE

missing items—a squealing, little _____, a bucket filled with
                                         NOUN

_____, and a signal flag to guide the _____ sailing
TYPE OF LIQUID   PLURAL NOUN

into the harbor. You'll want to avoid the eight-legged _____.
                                                            NOUN

There's also a/an _____ giant. The bucket is hidden among
                       ADJECTIVE

the _____ growing in the giant's garden, but as long as
      TYPE OF FOOD (PLURAL)

you give him a Golden _____, he'll let you enter.
                           NOUN

Abby: Giants and spiders and _____—oh my! Any final tips
                                       PLURAL NOUN

for our audience?

Pilgrim: Look for a/an _____ jet pack. Just strap it on your
                               ADJECTIVE

_____ and away you'll _____!
PART OF THE BODY   VERB

MAD LIBS® is fun to play with friends, but you can also play it by yourself! To begin with, DO NOT look at the story on the page below. Fill in the blanks on this page with the words called for. Then, using the words you have selected, fill in the blank spaces in the story.

Now you've created your own hilarious MAD LIBS® game!

SHARK TOOTH ISLAND: A QUEST WITH BITE

FIRST NAME (MALE) _____

ADJECTIVE _____

NOUN _____

A PLACE _____

VERB _____

NOUN _____

ADJECTIVE _____

PERSON IN ROOM _____

NOUN _____

PLURAL NOUN _____

VERB ENDING IN "ING" _____

ADJECTIVE _____

ARTICLE OF CLOTHING _____

NOUN _____

TYPE OF LIQUID _____

PLURAL NOUN _____

PART OF THE BODY (PLURAL) _____

My name is Professor _____ Hammerhead, and I'm a/an
            FIRST NAME (MALE)

_____ shark expert. I've been studying the Great Booga, a
  ADJECTIVE

man-eating _____ that has terrorized (the) _____
         NOUN   A PLACE

for years, making it unsafe to _____ in the waters here! It's
                      VERB

my greatest hope that some brave _____—such as the clever
                        NOUN

and _____ adventurer _____—will discover how to
   ADJECTIVE   PERSON IN ROOM

outsmart the Great Booga and save me from this deserted

_____ where I am stranded. The key is to find the Medicine
 NOUN

Man who lives near the ancient _____. He can make a/an
                     PLURAL NOUN

_____ potion to put the shark to sleep. But the Medicine
VERB ENDING IN "ING"

Man will only talk to you if you look like a/an _____ native,
                             ADJECTIVE

so you will need to wear a grass-covered _____. Then
                      ARTICLE OF CLOTHING

he'll reveal the ingredients for the potion: a bone from a prehistoric

_____, some _____ from a coconut, and the secret
  NOUN   TYPE OF LIQUID

ingredient: a mixture resembling creamed _____. I shall keep
                     PLURAL NOUN

my _____ crossed that I'll be rescued soon!
PART OF THE BODY (PLURAL)

MAD LIBS® is fun to play with friends, but you can also play it by yourself! To begin with, DO NOT look at the story on the page below. Fill in the blanks on this page with the words called for. Then, using the words you have selected, fill in the blank spaces in the story.

Now you've created your own hilarious MAD LIBS® game!

TIME TANGLED ISLAND: TIME TRAVELER WANTED

ADJECTIVE _____

PART OF THE BODY (PLURAL) _____

PLURAL NOUN _____

ADJECTIVE _____

PLURAL NOUN _____

PLURAL NOUN _____

VERB _____

ADJECTIVE _____

PLURAL NOUN _____

ADJECTIVE _____

CELEBRITY _____

NOUN _____

NUMBER _____

PLURAL NOUN _____

PART OF THE BODY _____

ADJECTIVE _____

VERB _____

PLURAL NOUN _____

MAD LIBS®
TIME TANGLED ISLAND: TIME TRAVELER WANTED

Are you smart, _____, and exceptionally skilled with your
                  ADJECTIVE

_____? Do you crave action, adventure, and
PART OF THE BODY (PLURAL)

_____? Then *you* could be a time traveler! The future has
   PLURAL NOUN

become a/an _____ wasteland covered with ruined
                 ADJECTIVE

_____. Join our elite team as we return misplaced
   PLURAL NOUN

_____ to the correct periods in history. _____ with
   PLURAL NOUN   VERB

Viking warriors, climb _____ pyramids, and leap over pits of
                            ADJECTIVE

twisting, poisonous _____. Although experience is not
                         PLURAL NOUN

required, priority will be given to those with knowledge of

_____ historical figures, like Declaration of Independence
   ADJECTIVE

author, _____. Time-traveling gear—including a gold pocket
            CELEBRITY

_____—is provided. Starting salary is _____
         NOUN   NUMBER

_____ per week. If you have your _____ set on a
   PLURAL NOUN   PART OF THE BODY

bright and _____ future, then the job of time traveler might
                ADJECTIVE

be right for you. _____ today for an application! Only
                       VERB

qualified _____ need apply.
               PLURAL NOUN

From POPTROPICA MAD LIBS® • © 2007–2012 Pearson Education, Inc. All rights reserved. Published in 2012 by Price Stern Sloan, a division of Penguin Young Readers Group, 345 Hudson Street, New York, NY 10014.

MAD LIBS® is fun to play with friends, but you can also play it by yourself! To begin with, DO NOT look at the story on the page below. Fill in the blanks on this page with the words called for. Then, using the words you have selected, fill in the blank spaces in the story.

Now you've created your own hilarious MAD LIBS® game!

24 CARROT ISLAND:
INSIDE THE MIND OF A VILLAIN

ADJECTIVE _____

PART OF THE BODY (PLURAL) _____

NOUN _____

NOUN _____

PLURAL NOUN _____

ADJECTIVE _____

A PLACE _____

PLURAL NOUN _____

NOUN _____

TYPE OF LIQUID _____

NOUN _____

ADJECTIVE _____

PART OF THE BODY (PLURAL) _____

NOUN _____

VERB _____

MAD LIBS
24 CARROT ISLAND:
INSIDE THE MIND OF A VILLAIN

I, Dr. Hare, have hatched a bold and _____ plot to take over
_____ ADJECTIVE

the world and control the _____ of all mankind! I
_____ PART OF THE BODY (PLURAL)

may not look like your traditional evil _____, but do not
_____ NOUN

underestimate me! Yes, I may hop around dressed as a large pink

_____ with green goggles, rabbit ears, and oversize
NOUN

_____ jutting from my mouth, but I have a/an
PLURAL NOUN

_____ brain the size of (the) _____—and I know
ADJECTIVE   A PLACE

how to use it! Once I steal all the _____ growing on 24
_____ PLURAL NOUN

Carrot Island, I will use the Island's _____ Factory to
_____ NOUN

convert them into carrot-flavored _____ to use as fuel in my
_____ TYPE OF LIQUID

_____-shaped spaceship. The townspeople of the Island
NOUN

will be powerless to stop me! I will kidnap them, force them to

wear my super-_____ bunny-ear helmets on their
_____ ADJECTIVE

_____, and turn them into my _____
PART OF THE BODY (PLURAL)   NOUN

Drones who will do whatever I command. I can promise you this: I

will take over the world or _____ trying! Beware—or be hare!
VERB

From POPTROPICA MAD LIBS® • © 2007–2012 Pearson Education, Inc. All rights reserved. Published in 2012
by Price Stern Sloan, a division of Penguin Young Readers Group, 345 Hudson Street, New York, NY 10014.

MAD LIBS® is fun to play with friends, but you can also play it by yourself! To begin with, DO NOT look at the story on the page below. Fill in the blanks on this page with the words called for. Then, using the words you have selected, fill in the blank spaces in the story.

Now you've created your own hilarious MAD LIBS® game!

SUPER POWER ISLAND: THE POWERS-THAT-BE-EVIL

PART OF THE BODY (PLURAL) _____

PLURAL NOUN _____

PART OF THE BODY _____

PLURAL NOUN _____

VERB _____

PLURAL NOUN _____

PLURAL NOUN _____

NOUN _____

ADJECTIVE _____

VERB _____

PLURAL NOUN _____

PLURAL NOUN _____

TYPE OF LIQUID _____

PART OF THE BODY _____

MAD LIBS
SUPER POWER ISLAND:
THE POWERS-THAT-BE-EVIL

The people of Super Power Island are scared out of their

_____. Escaped _____ with dangerous
PART OF THE BODY (PLURAL)   PLURAL NOUN

powers are on the loose! Beware of these bad guys:

• **Sir Rebral**—This creep uses the power of his _____ to toss
                                     PART OF THE BODY

  heavy _____ around like they're pebbles. To stop him,
         PLURAL NOUN

  _____ up and down like crazy—those _____ will
     VERB   PLURAL NOUN

  fly back at him and knock him out.

• **Crusher**—This junkyard rogue uses his superstrength to heave

  _____ at his opponents. Use the junkyard's mechanical
    PLURAL NOUN

  _____ to crush this _____ madman.
     NOUN   ADJECTIVE

• **Betty Jetty**—She possesses the power of flight, so you can't battle

  her unless you can _____, too! Watch out for the green
                   VERB

  energy _____ that she'll fire at you.
        PLURAL NOUN

• **Ratman**—This stinky, sewer-dwelling scoundrel surrounds himself

  with buzzing, biting _____. Douse him with a forceful
                  PLURAL NOUN

  blast of _____ to knock him on his _____.
     TYPE OF LIQUID   PART OF THE BODY

From POPTROPICA MAD LIBS® • © 2007–2012 Pearson Education, Inc. All rights reserved. Published in 2012
by Price Stern Sloan, a division of Penguin Young Readers Group, 345 Hudson Street, New York, NY 10014.

MAD LIBS® is fun to play with friends, but you can also play it by yourself! To begin with, DO NOT look at the story on the page below. Fill in the blanks on this page with the words called for. Then, using the words you have selected, fill in the blank spaces in the story.

Now you've created your own hilarious MAD LIBS® game!

SPY ISLAND: TOOLS OF THE TRADE

ADJECTIVE _____

PLURAL NOUN _____

PART OF THE BODY (PLURAL) _____

PERSON IN ROOM _____

ADJECTIVE _____

CELEBRITY _____

ADJECTIVE _____

VERB ENDING IN "ING" _____

NOUN _____

ADJECTIVE _____

PLURAL NOUN _____

ARTICLE OF CLOTHING _____

ADJECTIVE _____

NOUN _____

SAME NOUN _____

PART OF THE BODY (PLURAL) _____

PLURAL NOUN _____

MAD LIBS®
SPY ISLAND:
TOOLS OF THE TRADE

The evil minds behind B.A.D.—which stands for Bald and

_____—are using powerful laser _____ to vaporize
　　ADJECTIVE　　　　　　　　　　　　　　　　PLURAL NOUN

the hair from the _____ of unsuspecting citizens.
　　　　　　　　PART OF THE BODY (PLURAL)

Agent _____ must foil B.A.D.'s plans using these
　　　　PERSON IN ROOM

_____gadgets:
　ADJECTIVE

- **Chameleon Suit**—Created by operative _____, this
　　　　　　　　　　　　　　　　　　　　　　　CELEBRITY

_____outfit lets an agent blend in to his surroundings as
　ADJECTIVE

long as he's not _____at all.
　　　　　　VERB ENDING IN "ING"

- **Laser Pen**—This ordinary-looking _____ helps an agent
　　　　　　　　　　　　　　　　　NOUN

gain entry to off-limits places by cutting through _____
　　　　　　　　　　　　　　　　　　　　　　ADJECTIVE

metal bars on windows, gates, or _____.
　　　　　　　　　　　　　PLURAL NOUN

- **Grappling Bowtie**—Fashioned to look like a/an _____,
　　　　　　　　　　　　　　　　　　　　ARTICLE OF CLOTHING

this _____ gadget lets an agent swing from _____
　　ADJECTIVE　　　　　　　　　　　　　　　　NOUN

to _____like Spider-Man.
　SAME NOUN

- **Ultra Vision Goggles**—Agents put these over their

_____ to see anything from invisible _____
PART OF THE BODY (PLURAL)　　　　　　　　　　　PLURAL NOUN

to the color of someone's underwear.

From POPTROPICA MAD LIBS® • © 2007–2012 Pearson Education, Inc. All rights reserved. Published in 2012 by Price Stern Sloan, a division of Penguin Young Readers Group, 345 Hudson Street, New York, NY 10014.

MAD LIBS® is fun to play with friends, but you can also play it by yourself! To begin with, DO NOT look at the story on the page below. Fill in the blanks on this page with the words called for. Then, using the words you have selected, fill in the blank spaces in the story.

Now you've created your own hilarious MAD LIBS® game!

ASTRO KNIGHTS ISLAND: THE FINAL BATTLE

ADJECTIVE _____

VERB ENDING IN "ING" _____

CELEBRITY (FEMALE) _____

PLURAL NOUN _____

PERSON IN ROOM (MALE) _____

TYPE OF FOOD _____

ARTICLE OF CLOTHING _____

COLOR _____

ANIMAL _____

ADJECTIVE _____

PLURAL NOUN _____

NOUN _____

ADJECTIVE _____

VERB _____

PART OF THE BODY (PLURAL) _____

ADJECTIVE _____

ADJECTIVE _____

MAD LIBS

ASTRO KNIGHTS ISLAND: THE FINAL BATTLE

This is ace reporter Ollie Tweeterdorf of WPOP Channel 4 with

a/an _____ news update. I'm _____ here
    ADJECTIVE   VERB ENDING IN "ING"

outside the Crystal Gate where _____, the Princess of
                      CELEBRITY (FEMALE)

Arturus, is being held captive by the wicked Mordred. Her knight in

shining _____, _____, along with his three
     PLURAL NOUN   PERSON IN ROOM (MALE)

loyal companions—Sir _____, Sir Itchy _____,
              TYPE OF FOOD   ARTICLE OF CLOTHING

and Sir _____ _____—has just rushed inside to
      COLOR   ANIMAL

save her. They reportedly found Mordred wearing a/an

_____ robot suit and throwing exploding black
  ADJECTIVE

_____. Merlin, the mechanical flying _____ and
  PLURAL NOUN   NOUN

trusty sidekick of the knights, tried to deflect the bombs but got

zapped. Things are not looking _____ for our heroes! Can
                       ADJECTIVE

Mordred be stopped? Will Merlin _____ again? Do the
                     VERB

knights' tights make their _____ look big? For the
               PART OF THE BODY (PLURAL)

answers to these and other _____ questions about this
                ADJECTIVE

developing story, stay tuned to this _____ channel!
                ADJECTIVE

From POPTROPICA MAD LIBS® • © 2007–2012 Pearson Education, Inc. All rights reserved. Published in 2012
by Price Stern Sloan, a division of Penguin Young Readers Group, 345 Hudson Street, New York, NY 10014.

MAD LIBS® is fun to play with friends, but you can also play it by yourself! To begin with, DO NOT look at the story on the page below. Fill in the blanks on this page with the words called for. Then, using the words you have selected, fill in the blank spaces in the story.

Now you've created your own hilarious MAD LIBS® game!

COUNTERFEIT ISLAND: THE ART OF THE STEAL

NOUN _____

A PLACE _____

ADJECTIVE _____

PLURAL NOUN _____

ADJECTIVE _____

ADJECTIVE _____

PERSON IN ROOM (FEMALE) _____

NOUN _____

PLURAL NOUN _____

VERB ENDING IN "ING" _____

VERB _____

PLURAL NOUN _____

NOUN _____

PART OF THE BODY _____

ARTICLE OF CLOTHING _____

VERB _____

NOUN _____

MAD LIBS

COUNTERFEIT ISLAND: THE ART OF THE STEAL

The Black _____, the greatest art thief in all of (the)
              NOUN

_____, has stolen _____ masterpieces from famous
   A PLACE   ADJECTIVE

museums like the Metropolitan Museum of _____ in New
                                              PLURAL NOUN

York. Here are her tips for pulling off a/an _____ heist:
                                                  ADJECTIVE

1. Identify a/an _____, valuable painting to steal, like the *Mona*
                   ADJECTIVE

_____ by the legendary Italian _____,
PERSON IN ROOM (FEMALE)   NOUN

Leonardo da Vinci.

2. Gain access to the gallery by crawling through underground

_____.
  PLURAL NOUN

3. Avoid laser beams by ducking and _____.
                                     VERB ENDING IN "ING"

4. _____ in complete silence; otherwise, you'll activate the
      VERB

alarm—and security _____ with guns will come running!
                      PLURAL NOUN

5. Use a magnifying _____ to inspect the painting with your
                        NOUN

_____.
PART OF THE BODY

6. Tuck the artwork securely inside your _____.
                                          ARTICLE OF CLOTHING

7. _____ as fast as you can to the getaway _____
      VERB   NOUN

parked outside.

MAD LIBS® is fun to play with friends, but you can also play it by yourself! To begin with, DO NOT look at the story on the page below. Fill in the blanks on this page with the words called for. Then, using the words you have selected, fill in the blank spaces in the story.

Now you've created your own hilarious MAD LIBS® game!

REALITY TV ISLAND: GAME ON

ADJECTIVE _____

PERSON IN ROOM _____

NOUN _____

NOUN _____

PART OF THE BODY _____

NOUN _____

ADJECTIVE _____

VERB _____

TYPE OF LIQUID _____

PART OF THE BODY (PLURAL) _____

VERB _____

NOUN _____

PLURAL NOUN _____

PLURAL NOUN _____

PART OF THE BODY (PLURAL) _____

NOUN _____

MAD☺LIBS®
REALITY TV ISLAND: GAME ON

Can you face popular reality TV contestants like _____
ADJECTIVE

_____ and not get voted off the _____? To take
PERSON IN ROOM   _NOUN_

home the show's grand _____, just beat these challenges:
NOUN

- **Boulder Push**—You'll need plenty of upper _____
  PART OF THE BODY

  strength for this challenge! Be the first to push your huge

  _____ across the finish line.
  NOUN

- **Geyser Guess**—Are you feeling _____? Hopefully luck
  ADJECTIVE

  will be with you as you carefully choose where to _____.
  VERB

  Otherwise, a rush of _____ will explode beneath your
  TYPE OF LIQUID

  _____ and send you flying!
  PART OF THE BODY (PLURAL)

- **Hang Glider**—_____ across the sky with the grace and
  VERB

  speed of a flying _____ while avoiding erupting
  NOUN

  _____ and swooping _____.
  PLURAL NOUN   _PLURAL NOUN_

- **Mountain Race**—Are you fast on your _____?
  PART OF THE BODY (PLURAL)

  Reach the top of the towering _____ before your
  NOUN

  opponents do.

From POPTROPICA MAD LIBS® • © 2007–2012 Pearson Education, Inc. All rights reserved. Published in 2012
by Price Stern Sloan, a division of Penguin Young Readers Group, 345 Hudson Street, New York, NY 10014.

MAD LIBS® is fun to play with friends, but you can also play it by yourself! To begin with, DO NOT look at the story on the page below. Fill in the blanks on this page with the words called for. Then, using the words you have selected, fill in the blank spaces in the story.

Now you've created your own hilarious MAD LIBS® game!

MYTHOLOGY ISLAND: AGAINST ALL GODS

NOUN _____

PERSON IN ROOM (MALE) _____

PLURAL NOUN _____

NOUN _____

NOUN _____

TYPE OF LIQUID _____

NOUN _____

PART OF THE BODY _____

ADJECTIVE _____

PART OF THE BODY (PLURAL) _____

NOUN _____

PLURAL NOUN _____

VERB _____

CELEBRITY (MALE) _____

NOUN _____

MAD LIBS

MYTHOLOGY ISLAND: AGAINST ALL GODS

Oops! You picked a Golden _____ off a fruit tree and made
NOUN

_____, the king of the Greek gods, very angry. Luckily,
PERSON IN ROOM (MALE)

he promises to spare your life if you retrieve these five items listed on

the Sacred _____ Scroll:
PLURAL NOUN

- A colorful _____ growing in the Garden of the Sphinx,
NOUN

 who is half woman, half _____. She'll give it to you if you
NOUN

 can get _____ flowing to her garden.
TYPE OF LIQUID

- A golden ring belonging to the half-human, half-_____
NOUN

 Minotaur. The ring is easy to locate—it's (unfortunately) in the

 _____ of this _____ creature.
PART OF THE BODY   ADJECTIVE

- A scale from the Hydra, a sea beast with five _____!
PART OF THE BODY (PLURAL)

- A giant pearl located inside a huge _____ within the
NOUN

 Kingdom of Poseidon, god of the _____. To succeed, you
PLURAL NOUN

 need to be able to _____ underwater for a while.
VERB

- A whisker from _____, guardian of the Underworld. He
CELEBRITY (MALE)

 may be a three-headed dog, but beware—man's best _____
NOUN

he is *not*!

From POPTROPICA MAD LIBS® • © 2007–2012 Pearson Education, Inc. All rights reserved. Published in 2012
by Price Stern Sloan, a division of Penguin Young Readers Group, 345 Hudson Street, New York, NY 10014.

MAD LIBS® is fun to play with friends, but you can also play it by yourself! To begin with, DO NOT look at the story on the page below. Fill in the blanks on this page with the words called for. Then, using the words you have selected, fill in the blank spaces in the story.

Now you've created your own hilarious MAD LIBS® game!

SKULLDUGGERY ISLAND: AN ODE TO PIRATES

PLURAL NOUN _____

ADJECTIVE _____

VERB ENDING IN "ING" _____

ADJECTIVE _____

NOUN _____

CELEBRITY _____

VERB _____

VERB _____

ADJECTIVE _____

PART OF THE BODY _____

ADJECTIVE _____

PLURAL NOUN _____

PERSON IN ROOM _____

NOUN _____

MAD LIBS

SKULLDUGGERY ISLAND: AN ODE TO PIRATES

Aye, shiver me _____ and raise the pirate flag
              PLURAL NOUN

To our crew of _____ scalawags!
           ADJECTIVE

Swashbuckling and _____ we do with pleasure
               VERB ENDING IN "ING"

As we sail the _____ seas for treasure.
            ADJECTIVE

With the evil _____ Captain _____ at our wheel,
           NOUN   **CELEBRITY**

We'll plunder, pillage, _____, and steal!
                 VERB

And just when you think it's time for a rest,

We'll _____ upon a/an _____ man's chest!
      VERB   **ADJECTIVE**

So strap on your _____ patch and away we'll go,
             PART OF THE BODY

While chanting a/an _____ "Yo-Ho-Ho!"
              ADJECTIVE

But if you lily-livered _____ won't join our song,
             PLURAL NOUN

We'll make _____ walk the _____ at dawn!
      PERSON IN ROOM   **NOUN**

From POPTROPICA MAD LIBS® • © 2007–2012 Pearson Education, Inc. All rights reserved. Published in 2012
by Price Stern Sloan, a division of Penguin Young Readers Group, 345 Hudson Street, New York, NY 10014.

MAD LIBS® is fun to play with friends, but you can also play it by yourself! To begin with, DO NOT look at the story on the page below. Fill in the blanks on this page with the words called for. Then, using the words you have selected, fill in the blank spaces in the story.

Now you've created your own hilarious MAD LIBS® game!

STEAMWORKS ISLAND: MECH CHECK

ADJECTIVE _____

PLURAL NOUN _____

ADJECTIVE _____

NOUN _____

NOUN _____

ANIMAL _____

ADJECTIVE _____

PART OF THE BODY (PLURAL) _____

VERB _____

PLURAL NOUN _____

PLURAL NOUN _____

PLURAL NOUN _____

PART OF THE BODY (PLURAL) _____

NOUN _____

TYPE OF LIQUID _____

ADJECTIVE _____

MAD LIBS®
STEAMWORKS ISLAND: MECH CHECK

The people of Steamworks Island have disappeared under _____
                                                        ADJECTIVE

circumstances. Evil plantlike _____ lurk around every corner.
                               PLURAL NOUN

Only a giant, _____ robot called a Mech can save the day. Here
              ADJECTIVE

are step-by-_____ instructions for assembling one:
            NOUN

1. Drop in a turbocharged steam _____ to boost the Mech's
                                 NOUN

   _____-power.
     ANIMAL

2. Install a/an _____ crank to make the robot's _____
                ADJECTIVE   PART OF THE BODY (PLURAL)

   move back and forth so it can walk, run, and even _____.
                                                      VERB

3. Tighten all the nuts, bolts, gears, _____, and _____
                                        PLURAL NOUN   PLURAL NOUN

   so the Mech stays firmly together.

4. Oil the joints with _____ to make sure the Mech can
                        PLURAL NOUN

   bend easily, especially at its _____.
                                  PART OF THE BODY (PLURAL)

5. Attach the _____ Blaster and fill it with toxic _____
               NOUN   TYPE OF LIQUID

   to spray the _____ plant monsters.
                 ADJECTIVE

MAD LIBS® is fun to play with friends, but you can also play it by yourself! To begin with, DO NOT look at the story on the page below. Fill in the blanks on this page with the words called for. Then, using the words you have selected, fill in the blank spaces in the story.

Now you've created your own hilarious MAD LIBS® game!

CRYPTIDS ISLAND: UNCOVER THE EVIDENCE

PLURAL NOUN _____

ADJECTIVE _____

NOUN _____

NOUN _____

TYPE OF LIQUID _____

NOUN _____

NOUN _____

PART OF THE BODY _____

PART OF THE BODY _____

ADJECTIVE _____

NOUN _____

PART OF THE BODY _____

NOUN _____

PART OF THE BODY _____

PLURAL NOUN _____

NOUN _____

ANIMAL (PLURAL) _____

PART OF THE BODY (PLURAL) _____

MAD☺LIBS®
CRYPTIDS ISLAND:
UNCOVER THE EVIDENCE

An eccentric billionaire is offering a reward of one million

_____ for proof that these four cryptids—_____
PLURAL NOUN   ADJECTIVE

creatures that may or may not be real—actually do exist:

- **Loch Ness** _____—This sea _____ lives in the
  NOUN   NOUN

  calm blue _____ of Loch _____ in Scotland.
  TYPE OF LIQUID   NOUN

  Playing music on a/an _____ will cause the long _____
  NOUN   PART OF THE BODY

  of the monster to stretch up from the lake's depths.

- **Big-**_____—Also called the Yeti, this _____
  PART OF THE BODY   ADJECTIVE

  creature resembles a hairy, bearded _____. To track him,
  NOUN

  follow his large, deep _____ prints.
  PART OF THE BODY

- **Jersey Devil**—This winged _____ has two horns poking
  NOUN

  out from its _____ and two gleaming yellow
  PART OF THE BODY

  _____ that help it see.
  PLURAL NOUN

- **Chupacabra**—This nasty four-legged _____ likes to eat
  NOUN

  spotted _____ and has a growl that will make your
  ANIMAL (PLURAL)

  _____ stand on end!
  PART OF THE BODY (PLURAL)

MAD LIBS® is fun to play with friends, but you can also play it by yourself! To begin with, DO NOT look at the story on the page below. Fill in the blanks on this page with the words called for. Then, using the words you have selected, fill in the blank spaces in the story.

Now you've created your own hilarious MAD LIBS® game!

WILD WEST ISLAND: HARNESS YOUR INNER COWBOY

ADJECTIVE _____

NOUN _____

ADJECTIVE _____

NOUN _____

PLURAL NOUN _____

NOUN _____

ANIMAL _____

PART OF THE BODY _____

TYPE OF FOOD _____

VERB ENDING IN "ING" _____

ADJECTIVE _____

PERSON IN ROOM (FEMALE) _____

PLURAL NOUN _____

ANIMAL _____

PART OF THE BODY _____

PLURAL NOUN _____

NOUN _____

MAD LIBS®
WILD WEST ISLAND:
HARNESS YOUR INNER COWBOY

Are you _____ enough to pin a marshal's star-shaped
            ADJECTIVE

_____ on your chest and go after El Mustachio Grande—
     NOUN

whose name means "_____ _____"—and his gang
                       ADJECTIVE   NOUN

of wild _____? To become the best cow-_____ in
          PLURAL NOUN   NOUN

the West, you need to:

• tame a wild _____ by remaining firmly seated on its
                 ANIMAL

_____ while it tries to throw you off,
PART OF THE BODY

• compete with a/an _____ shooter in a/an _____
                       TYPE OF FOOD   VERB ENDING IN "ING"

contest against _____ sharpshooters like Miss
                    ADJECTIVE

_____ Oakley,
PERSON IN ROOM (FEMALE)

• get a coil of _____ and lasso a missing _____
                  PLURAL NOUN   ANIMAL

• win at cards in a casino by slapping your _____ down
                                               PART OF THE BODY

whenever you see a jack—then take all the _____ in the
                                              PLURAL NOUN

stack, and

• use a gold pan to sift through dirt until you find a sparkly Gold

_____ to trade.
     NOUN

MAD LIBS® is fun to play with friends, but you can also play it by yourself! To begin with, DO NOT look at the story on the page below. Fill in the blanks on this page with the words called for. Then, using the words you have selected, fill in the blank spaces in the story.

Now you've created your own hilarious MAD LIBS® game!

SHRINK RAY ISLAND: THINK BIG TO WIN

ADJECTIVE _____

NOUN _____

NOUN _____

ADJECTIVE _____

NOUN _____

NOUN _____

ADJECTIVE _____

NOUN _____

NOUN _____

TYPE OF LIQUID _____

ADJECTIVE _____

VERB _____

ADJECTIVE _____

NOUN _____

CJ, the _____ pupil at the school science fair, is missing—

ADJECTIVE

along with her genius invention, a shrink ray _____. When I

NOUN

go to her apartment to find her, I get blasted by a masked

_____ carrying the shrink ray. Whoa! I'm so tiny that I

NOUN

almost get crushed by the _____ paws of CJ's pet

ADJECTIVE

_____! I find the shrink ray blueprints and a piece of paper

NOUN

with a secret message that says to look for CJ through her tele-

_____. She's inside the school hiding from Mr. Silva, her

NOUN

science teacher, who is the _____ thief! I flush the blueprints

ADJECTIVE

down the _____, jump into a toy _____, and speed

NOUN   NOUN

to the school. Mr. Silva tries to shrink me into oblivion, but I hide

behind a mirror. The ray deflects back, hitting Mr. Silva—and he falls

into a/an _____ ant farm, never to be seen again! I flip the

ADJECTIVE

switch on the shrink ray gun to "_____," so CJ and I return

VERB

to our normal sizes. Not only are we lucky to be _____, but

ADJECTIVE

CJ even takes home the first-place _____ at the science fair.

NOUN

From POPTROPICA MAD LIBS® • © 2007–2012 Pearson Education, Inc. All rights reserved. Published in 2012
by Price Stern Sloan, a division of Penguin Young Readers Group, 345 Hudson Street, New York, NY 10014.

MAD LIBS® is fun to play with friends, but you can also play it by yourself! To begin with, DO NOT look at the story on the page below. Fill in the blanks on this page with the words called for. Then, using the words you have selected, fill in the blank spaces in the story.

Now you've created your own hilarious MAD LIBS® game!

MYSTERY TRAIN ISLAND:
ALL ABOARD FOR
A WHODUNIT ADVENTURE

ADJECTIVE _____

PLURAL NOUN _____

NOUN _____

PERSON IN ROOM (FEMALE) _____

TYPE OF FOOD _____

ADJECTIVE _____

VERB ENDING IN "ING" _____

PLURAL NOUN _____

PLURAL NOUN _____

NOUN _____

ADJECTIVE _____

PART OF THE BODY _____

VERB _____

NOUN _____

NOUN _____

MAD●LIBS®
MYSTERY TRAIN ISLAND:
ALL ABOARD FOR
A WHODUNIT ADVENTURE

A/An _____ crime has been committed aboard a train
　　　　ADJECTIVE

carrying _____ to the 1893 World's Fair in Chicago. A
　　　　PLURAL NOUN

transformer _____ that powers the Ferris wheel has been stolen!
　　　　NOUN

The thief turns out to be Mademoiselle _____, a
　　　　　　　　　　　　　　　　　　PERSON IN ROOM (FEMALE)

reporter with the French newspaper *Le* _____. She wanted the
　　　　　　　　　　　　　　　　TYPE OF FOOD

fair to be held in her hometown of Paris. Now she's going to destroy

the _____ transformer and ruin the fair! She jumps off the
　　　ADJECTIVE

train and takes off _____ through the fairgrounds. You
　　　　　　　　VERB ENDING IN "ING"

give chase, running past attractions like ferocious-looking _____
　　　　　　　　　　　　　　　　　　　　　　　　　　　PLURAL NOUN

with large teeth and jugglers with flaming _____. You follow
　　　　　　　　　　　　　　　　　　PLURAL NOUN

the reporter to the top of the Ferris _____ when—watch
　　　　　　　　　　　　　　　　NOUN

out!—she tries to push a/an _____ crate right on top of your
　　　　　　　　　　　　　ADJECTIVE

_____! Luckily, you _____ just in the nick of time. As
PART OF THE BODY　　　　VERB

she hurls the _____ toward the ground, you swing like Tarzan
　　　　　　NOUN

from a hanging _____ in time to catch it, saving the day—and
　　　　　　NOUN

the fair!

MAD LIBS® is fun to play with friends, but you can also play it by yourself! To begin with, DO NOT look at the story on the page below. Fill in the blanks on this page with the words called for. Then, using the words you have selected, fill in the blank spaces in the story.

Now you've created your own hilarious MAD LIBS® game!

GAME SHOW ISLAND: OVERRUN BY ROBOTS

ADJECTIVE _____

PERSON IN ROOM _____

PART OF THE BODY _____

PLURAL NOUN _____

PART OF THE BODY _____

VERB _____

PLURAL NOUN _____

PLURAL NOUN _____

PLURAL NOUN _____

VERB _____

NOUN _____

CELEBRITY _____

VERB ENDING IN "ING" _____

ADJECTIVE _____

NOUN _____

NOUN _____

PART OF THE BODY _____

MAD LIBS
GAME SHOW ISLAND: OVERRUN BY ROBOTS

_____ robots overtook Game Show Island years ago. Their
ADJECTIVE

leader, a rogue robot named _____, rules with an iron
PERSON IN ROOM

_____! To restore humans to their rightful place, you need
PART OF THE BODY

to beat these mechanical _____ at their own games.
PLURAL NOUN

- **Scaredy Pants**—In these _____-raising races against the
PART OF THE BODY

  clock, you need to _____ in a pool of _____
  VERB   PLURAL NOUN

  to retrieve a Glow Stick without getting shocked by nasty

  _____ swimming below. You'll also sort rats, spiders, and
  PLURAL NOUN

  slimy _____ into bins and _____ carefully on a
  PLURAL NOUN   VERB

  tight rope without falling off.

- **Kerplunk**—Compete against two robots named Super

  _____ and _____ in obstacle courses that involve
  NOUN   CELEBRITY

  running, jumping, climbing, and _____.
  VERB ENDING IN "ING"

- **Mr. Yoshi's Super** _____ **Challenge**—Complete silly tasks
  ADJECTIVE

  like hatching out of an enormous _____ or being a human
  NOUN

  bowling _____. If Mr. Yoshi laughs his _____
  NOUN   PART OF THE BODY

  off, you win!

MAD LIBS® is fun to play with friends, but you can also play it by yourself! To begin with, DO NOT look at the story on the page below. Fill in the blanks on this page with the words called for. Then, using the words you have selected, fill in the blank spaces in the story.

Now you've created your own hilarious MAD LIBS® game!

GHOST STORY ISLAND: A SPIRITED MYSTERY

ADJECTIVE _____

NOUN _____

ADJECTIVE _____

PERSON IN ROOM (MALE) _____

PLURAL NOUN _____

ADJECTIVE _____

NOUN _____

PLURAL NOUN _____

NOUN _____

PART OF THE BODY _____

VERB _____

NOUN _____

PART OF THE BODY _____

ADJECTIVE _____

VERB _____

MAD☺LIBS®
GHOST STORY ISLAND:
A SPIRITED MYSTERY

Amid _____ reports that the secret of Ghost Story Island
ADJECTIVE

had finally been revealed, the Island's daily news-_____, the
NOUN

Hemlock Herald, published this _____ article:
ADJECTIVE

Famed ghost hunter _____ has solved the decades-
PERSON IN ROOM (MALE)

long mystery of the _____ haunting Hemlock Harbor. "Give
PLURAL NOUN

me a/an _____ thermal scanner and a/an _____
ADJECTIVE   NOUN

detector and I can prove—or disprove—the existence of anything,"

he says. It turns out two best _____ named Valiant Lovejoy
PLURAL NOUN

and Henry Flatbottom loved a/an _____ named Fiona.
NOUN

Valiant asked for her _____ in marriage. Not wanting to
PART OF THE BODY

_____ without Fiona, Henry forged a note from her to
VERB

Valiant saying she was in love with someone else and that he should

leave the Island. A devastated Valiant sailed off and died in a/an

_____-wreck. Fiona later died of a broken _____.
NOUN   PART OF THE BODY

Once Henry confessed his wrongdoing, the ghostly Fiona and Valiant

forgave him. The _____ couple can finally _____ in peace.
ADJECTIVE   VERB

From POPTROPICA MAD LIBS® • © 2007–2012 Pearson Education, Inc. All rights reserved. Published in 2012
by Price Stern Sloan, a division of Penguin Young Readers Group, 345 Hudson Street, New York, NY 10014.

MAD LIBS® is fun to play with friends, but you can also play it by yourself! To begin with, DO NOT look at the story on the page below. Fill in the blanks on this page with the words called for. Then, using the words you have selected, fill in the blank spaces in the story.

Now you've created your own hilarious MAD LIBS® game!

SOS ISLAND: CRUISING FOR TROUBLE

ADJECTIVE _____

NOUN _____

NOUN _____

VERB ENDING IN "ING" _____

TYPE OF LIQUID _____

NOUN _____

PLURAL NOUN _____

PART OF THE BODY _____

NOUN _____

ADJECTIVE _____

NOUN _____

PLURAL NOUN _____

TYPE OF LIQUID _____

ADJECTIVE _____

NOUN _____

CELEBRITY (MALE) _____

ADJECTIVE _____

NOUN _____

MAD LIBS
SOS ISLAND:
CRUISING FOR TROUBLE

It's like a/an _____ scene from a disaster movie! A cruise
            ADJECTIVE

ship on a/an _____-watching expedition strikes a massive
                NOUN

_____ and begins _____. As the ship fills with
   NOUN   VERB ENDING IN "ING"

_____, these passengers need to be rescued:
TYPE OF LIQUID

• A whale watcher wearing an inflatable life _____ and an "I
                                                    NOUN

   ♥ _____ " hat has gotten his _____ stuck in a pile
        PLURAL NOUN   PART OF THE BODY

of fallen debris.

• A crew member is swinging from a crystal _____ high up
                                                  NOUN

on the ceiling of the ship's _____ ballroom.
                                ADJECTIVE

• A mechanic trying to fix the ship with a/an _____ wrench
                                                    NOUN

is trapped because all of the _____ in the boiler room have
                                 PLURAL NOUN

burst and are shooting hot _____.
                              TYPE OF LIQUID

• The chef is stuck in the _____ freezer and has become a
                              ADJECTIVE

frozen _____-sicle.
          NOUN

• Captain _____ stubbornly remains at the ship's wheel.
            CELEBRITY (MALE)

A/an _____ captain must go down with his _____!
        ADJECTIVE   NOUN